THE LAST DAYS OF STEAM IN
SURREY
AND
SUSSEX

THE LAST DAYS OF STEAM IN

SURREY AND SUSSEX

– D. FEREDAY GLENN –

ALAN SUTTON
1989

ALAN SUTTON PUBLISHING
BRUNSWICK ROAD · GLOUCESTER · UK

ALAN SUTTON PUBLISHING INC
WOLFEBORO · NEW HAMPSHIRE · USA

First published 1989

British Library Cataloguing in Publication Data

Glenn, David Fereday
  Last days of steam in Surrey and Sussex
  1. South-east England. Steam locomotives.
  1953–1967 – Illustrations
  I. Title
  625.2'61'09422

  ISBN 0–86299–531–0

Library of Congress Cataloging in Publication Data applied for

Endpapers: Front: A 'Vulcan' class C2X No. 32521 working the Leatherhead to Guildford goods. Back: Class N 2-6-0 No. 31872 at the head of a mixed goods from Reading to Redhill, 10.1.62

Front Cover: The preserved Drummond T9 'Greyhound' 4-4-0 No. 120 passing over the points at Rudgwick while travelling between Guildford and Horsham, 24.6.62

Back Cover: A pair of Billinton 0-6-2T engines emerging from Midhurst tunnel, 24.6.62. The leading engine is No. 32417 (class E6), the other No. 32503 (class E4)

Typesetting and origination by
Alan Sutton Publishing Limited
Printed in Great Britain by
The Bath Press, Avon

Introduction

The railways of Surrey and Sussex are particularly interesting due to the extensive electrification undertaken between the two World Wars; also as the counties seem to be inextricably linked, it has been easier to treat them as a single entity.

The Portsmouth Direct line from Havant to Guildford and Woking (with the former branch from Petersfield to Midhurst and Pulborough) makes a convenient western boundary, while the main route from Basingstoke through Woking to Surbiton marks the northern extremity. On the eastern side the Tunbridge Wells to Hastings line forms a natural division, which incorporates the once independent KESR branch from Robertsbridge as far as Tenterden. The Coastway lines, centred on Brighton, provide a link across the whole of Sussex, while a short sequence from Havant to Hayling Island has also been included. Routes like the one between Reading and Redhill, via Guildford, are an important focus of attention: at one time a proliferation of secondary and branch lines criss-crossed the two counties. The area was served by a number of steam locomotive depots until 1967, and glimpses of them provide an ideal introduction to the rest of the book. It is worth bearing in mind that all three main constituents of the Southern Railway (which became the Southern Region of BR in 1948) were to be found in Surrey and Sussex. Perhaps this is why it was always so full of variety and interest to railway enthusiasts?

I am grateful to John Haydon, Dick Riley and Les Goff for the use of certain pictures; the remainder are from my own collection. Thanks are due to my son, Miles, for his help with the map. The recent rebuilding of Guildford station has rendered many scenes obsolete, while wholesale closures in the 1960s were accompanied by the relentless scrapping of steam locomotives. However, visitors to the Bluebell line can still enjoy a taste of the age of steam, and the Kent & East Sussex Railway is steadily extending towards Northiam and Bodiam.

David Fereday Glenn
1989

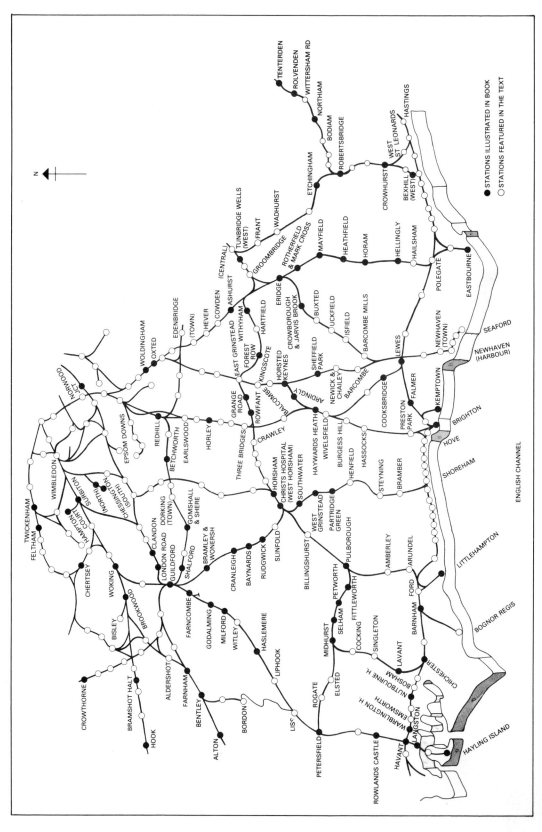

LAST DAYS OF STEAM IN SURREY & SUSSEX

● STATIONS ILLUSTRATED IN BOOK
○ STATIONS FEATURED IN THE TEXT

THE LAST DAYS OF STEAM IN

SURREY
AND
SUSSEX

Part 1: Locomotive Depots

A number of important depots in Surrey and Sussex provided engines for a variety of duties, from express passenger to shunting. The following were actually located in the two counties: 70C Guildford, Surrey; 74E St Leonards, Sussex; 75A Brighton, Sussex (sub-shed at Newhaven); 75B Redhill, Surrey; 75C Norwood Junction, Surrey; 75D Horsham, Sussex; 75E Three Bridges, Sussex; 75G Eastbourne, Sussex. Other depots serving the area, but just outside the county boundaries, included: 70B Feltham, Middlesex; 70D Basingstoke, Hampshire; 70E Reading, Berkshire; 71D (later 70F) Fratton, Hampshire; 74D Tonbridge, Kent; 75F Tunbridge Wells West, Kent.

Visiting engines from other Southern Region sheds were to be seen almost daily, and there was a regular Western Region duty from Reading to Redhill involving a 'Mogul' 2-6-0 or named 4-6-0s of the lightweight 'Manor' class. Weekend excursions brought Eastern Region class B1 4-6-0s to the South Coast on occasions, while visits from London Midland Region Stanier 'Black Five' 4-6-0s were almost routine. Of all the former constituent companies amalgamated into the Southern in 1923, the London Brighton & South Coast Railway had the most generous loading gauge, so the civil engineer was able to look kindly upon requests for an unusual locomotive to haul an excursion – as long as it only ran on the main line. This meant there was no impediment to a visit by the privately preserved Gresley Pacific, *Flying Scotsman*, via the Brighton line in 1966. By contrast, the former South Eastern & Chatham routes – in particular the Tonbridge to Hastings line and branches – were circumscribed with restrictions, hence the curious flat-sided coaching stock and narrow dimensions that afflicted design even in the diesel era.

Some impression of the unique atmosphere to be found at steam locomotive depots can be gained from the selection of pictures in these next few pages. Thanks to the generosity of a retired railwayman, Mr Les Goff, I have been able to include a handful of photographs taken at Littlehampton in the thirties, just prior to electrification. These give a fascinating insight into the heyday of steam on the Southern, offering a reminder of several types of engine that were commonplace then although none survive today. Because of the slightly more generous proportions of most former LBSCR locomotives, when the Brighton line and its ancillary routes were electrified it became difficult to find them alternative employment and few survived the early years of nationalization.

With track realignment and resignalling in progress in readiness for the end of steam on the Southern, veteran U class 2-6-0 No. 31791 clanks past the Guildford shed on 2.2.66 before passing beneath Farnham Road bridge. This engine had been built for the SECR as a 2-6-4T, but it was rebuilt as a tender locomotive by the Southern Railway in the late 1920s after the Riverhead accident had revealed instability at speed due to water slopping in the side tanks. The former depot site (70C) has been redeveloped as a multi-storey car park

Because of the cramped layout at Guildford, the coaling plant was built adjoining the station – although it was screened from the view of those on the platform. Some visiting engines, or those too large to be accommodated at the roundhouse, might be stored temporarily on the coal siding, as was the case with class H15 4-6-0 No. 30331 on 2.9.55. All six of the 30330–30335 batch of H15s were based at Salisbury (72B), being employed mostly on freight duties

Before the advent of diesel shunters, much of the yard work was carried out by Adams G6 0-6-0Ts. For some years Guildford was the home of No. 30349, seen here shunting wagons at the coaling stage on 7.8.55. Salisbury's No. 30331 can be discerned in the background, waiting to return to Woking yard

Another look at the coaling stage, this time from the cattle dock. Standard class 5MT 4-6-0 No. 73110 (for a time named *The Red Knight*) has been given the task of shunting coal wagons into position under the stage while Q1 0-6-0 No. 33006 receives attention over the ash pit. Another Standard engine shunts a wagon containing hot ash alongside the Bulleid. Although Guildford shed remained operational until the end of steam, the selection of motive power was much reduced by 2.2.66

The tradition of a four-coupled tank to shunt locos around Guildford roundhouse was maintained until the 1960s. The incumbent on 5.2.62 was class B4 0-4-0T No. 30089, built by the LSWR in November 1892 and named *Trouville* when based in Southampton Docks. Although nearly seventy years old, Guildford shed cleaners seem to have found time to give it the occasional wipe over with an oily rag. When withdrawn in 1963 it was replaced by a short-wheelbase USA 0-6-0T.

From 1908 onwards most of the Billinton class C2 0-6-0 goods engines were steadily reboilered with the bigger C3 type, thus becoming the C2x 'Large Vulcans'. No. 32437 was on shed at Brighton (75A) on 15.1.56, looking very smart in plain black after recent attention at the works. One of the Brighton-built 4MT 2-6-4T engines (No. 42087) can be seen behind. These were designed by Fairburn for the LMS (London Midland Region of British Railways) but were used initially on passenger duties all over Sussex to replace ageing I3 tanks

Even after being reboilered by Maunsell in the late 1920s, the small 4-4-2T engines of class I1x could hardly be called a runaway success; few, if any, lasted long enough to be given their BR numbers and insignia. No. 2002 (allocated BR number No. 32002) was being shunted within sight of Brighton station on 1.7.51, but did not last out the year

R.C. Riley

One of the rarely photographed 3-cylinder 'Mogul' locomotives of class N1, No. 31877, seen here in light steam over the ash pit at Brighton shed on Saturday, 10.6.61. In the background can be seen the former works shunter (DS377), which returned to capital stock as No. 32635 in 1959 and retained the traditional livery of Stroudley's improved engine green until withdrawal

The last survivors of classes E5 and E5x were taken out of service in 1956. Examples of both types of 0-6-2T, which had 5 ft 6 in driving wheels, were found dumped awaiting scrap at the back of Brighton shed on 15.1.56. Class E5 No. 32571 never received the mixed-traffic lining that was its due, but remained close to its original appearance when withdrawn after fifty years' work

Glinting in the bright sunshine, class H2 Atlantic No. 32426 *St Albans Head* had a full tender of coal at its home shed on 20.5.56. Sadly, it was taken out of service soon afterwards and, within two years, no 4-4-2 tender engines were left at work on any part of British Railways

Developed from Stroudley's 'West Brighton' design of 0-6-2T, the E3 class seldom made headlines. They mostly worked freight trains or performed shunting duties, in recognition of which they were painted unlined black in BR days. No. 32166 was still active at Brighton when pictured with an E4 near the coaling plant on 28.12.57

Brighton still boasted an octogenarian engine in the ornate Stroudley livery in 1961. No. 32635, formerly works shunter and numbered DS377, was in light steam on shed on 10 June to provide a splash of colour among the greys and blacks of other more modern motive power. As an Alx 0-6-0T, it was the only example to be painted like this when in service with BR and never obtained a cast smokebox numberplate. Had it lasted another year or two it might well have been preserved

One small engine that did find its way into preservation, eventually, was ex-SECR class P 0-6-0T No. 31556. It was at Brighton for some years doing light shunting and performing as shed pilot. On 28.12.57 it presented the visitor with an attractive broadside view silhouetted against the sheer cliff just outside the station. The tracks behind the locomotive are part of the Coastway West line to and from Portsmouth

The seventeen members of class K were the Brighton line's only 2-6-0 design, and were used principally on heavy freight work with some relief passenger duties in summer. No. 32353 was the last new loco to be built for the LBSCR in 1921; it looked spotless on shed, 7.10.62, while receiving some lubrication from a member of its crew. Again, sadly, none survived into preservation

Although since 1947 75A had had its own allocation of Bulleid Pacifics, it sometimes played host to visiting engines from other parts of the Southern. On 10.6.61 the rebuilt No. 34047 *Callington* joined a line of other locomotives waiting to be serviced in preparation for its return journey, proudly displaying a special headboard for a Dimplex works outing to the south coast resort. No. 34047 had an earlier association with Brighton for, as a new 'West Country' class 4-6-2, it was shedded there for working through trains to Bournemouth or Salisbury (for Plymouth or Cardiff)

These classic Brighton engines from the past were on display there on 7.10.62: the ninety-year old 'Terrier' No. 32636 (formerly *Fenchurch*) and Edwardian E6 0-6-2T No. 32418 were over the ash pit after completing a rail tour to Newhaven and back. The latter was still very much as built, whereas the little 0-6-0T had enlarged cylinders and the extended smokebox fitted to all Alx rebuilds. After working the very last train to Hayling Island in November 1963, No. 32636 was sold to the Bluebell Railway as a stablemate for *Stepney*. In November 1988 this splendid veteran of 1872 was repainted in BR lined-black livery – as depicted here – to recall the closure of the Hayling line twenty-five years before

Here the handsome 'Schools' class 4-4-0 No. 30928 *Stowe* can be seen being turned on the turntable at Redhill (75B) on 25.3.56, with headcode discs for Guildford and Reading displayed above the buffer beam. The Quarry Line, avoiding Redhill station and its complex junctions, runs at a lower level beyond the turntable. After a spell as a static exhibit at Beaulieu Motor Museum, this engine was transferred to the Bluebell Railway and was restored to active use during the 1980s

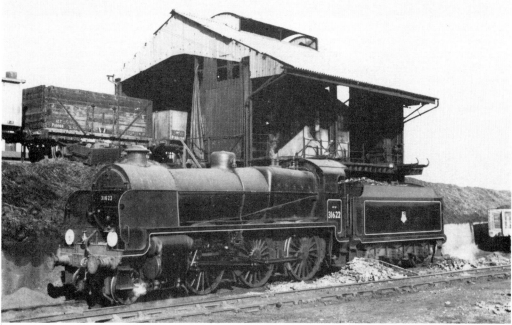

Framed by the coaling stage, class U 2-6-0 No. 31622 appeared to be in immaculate condition on 3.3.57 while being prepared for a Redhill to Reading service via Guildford. These useful engines, nicknamed 'U-Boats', could handle almost any kind of traffic and served the Southern well until the last days of steam; four examples have been preserved

In steam days Redhill was a fascinating junction, as it was one of the places where engines from some Kentish sheds could be seen. This former SECR class C 0-6-0 No. 31272 was based at Tonbridge (74D) for a number of years, but is seen here taking water from a distinctive Chatham water crane after bringing in a freight on 28.7.57. This robust Wainwright six-coupled design is represented today by another member of the class (once more than a hundred strong) at the Bluebell Railway in Sussex

A four-coupled express design that was modernized and improved by Maunsell in the 1920s, the D1 class of 4-4-0 performed excellently on the Kent coast routes until electrification. No. 31489 of Tonbridge shed is here being turned on Redhill turntable on 12.5.57. They all went for scrap, the last going in 1962

With no more than a surface coating of dust on its glossy black paintwork, 'Vulcan' class C2x 0-6-0 No. 32449 looked very smart idling with an ash truck in the shed yard at Redhill on 28.7.57. This type of engine was ideal for local pick-up goods duties all over the former LBSCR system, but cut down boiler mountings and a flatter style of dome casing were fitted in Southern days to allow them to work further afield when necessary

An unusual visitor to Redhill on 12.5.57 was a green-liveried 0-6-0 diesel-mechanical shunting locomotive, No. 11222. Fitted with a Gardner 8L3 engine which developed 204 bhp at 1,250 rpm, this machine had a five-speed gearbox and jackshaft drive; it was later renumbered D2252. Note the steam era headcode discs alongside the maker's own electric lighting. In the TOPS classification, this type was known as class 04

Norwood Junction shed (75C) provided a strange assortment of motive power to the enthusiast in the 1950s. There were some 'last survivors' from a forgotten past: Brighton 'Radials' that had been reboilered in the Edwardian period (using the I2 4-4-2T pattern) and original pre-war diesel shunters that had once been numbered 1–3. The visitor on 15.2.58 was offered a glimpse of both from the approach road. English Electric 0-6-0 No. 15203 of 1937 was a very different engine from the standard 350 bhp shunter, while class E4x 0-6-2T No. 32477 bore only a passing resemblance to the conventional E4

This close-up view of class E4x 0-6-2T No. 32477 shows the rather heavy frontal effect produced by reboilering, while the dome looks definitely non-standard – even home-made, perhaps? A normal N 2-6-0 brings up the rear at Norwood Junction, 15.2.58

Not all class E4x engines looked the same: No. 32466 had a neat profile, enhanced by a flush-fitting smokebox door. Seen here out of steam alongside Norwood Junction shed on 15.2.58, the small sub-class of reboilered engines was withdrawn in 1959

The smallest sub-class of all the reboilered Brighton 0-6-2Ts was the E6x which comprised just two locomotives. No. 32407 ended up with a double-domed boiler but was withdrawn in 1957, whereas No. 32411 had the normal C3-type boiler and survived until 1959. It is seen here in the shed yard at Norwood Junction on 15.2.58, taking water

Coaling facilities at Horsham depot (75D) were primitive, with a rail-mounted crane transferring fuel from a wagon into the engine's bunker or tender. On 29.6.59 class H 0-4-4T No. 31543 was being serviced before taking over a push–pull train at the station

The four-road shed at Tunbridge Wells West (75F) provided some of the motive power for trains to Oxted, Three Bridges, Tonbridge and Eastbourne. Sunday morning, 8.7.56, found the depot quite full: a Fairburn 4MT 2-6-4T was under repair on the track nearest the station, while former SECR 0-4-4Ts occupied the adjoining road. 'H' tanks Nos. 31543, 31278 and 31327 were in light steam in readiness for their next duties

The electrification of the Brighton main line and along the coast to Chichester and Portsmouth caused the closure of some small steam sheds and a great reduction in loco-hauled trains during the 1930s. The need for LBSCR tender engines, never very large due to relatively short distances between termini, became less following a temporary reprieve caused by World War II. This elegant class Hl Atlantic, No. 2041 *Peveril Point*, was an early casualty as it was withdrawn in 1944; it was photographed at Littlehampton in the mid-1930s (before electrification) painted in fully-lined olive green livery

D. Fereday Glenn collection, courtesy Mr L. Goff

Again in Littlehampton shed yard during the same period, before the onset of electrification, was one of the original Billinton class B4 4-4-0 locomotives; this type became noted for its express passenger role on the main line between London and Brighton. No. 2062 survived the war and was withdrawn after nationalization without receiving its BR number

D. Fereday Glenn collection, courtesy Mr L. Goff

The rebuilt 'B4x' engines looked to be thoroughly massive, modern machines. No. 2050 was alongside the shed at Littlehampton in the mid-1930s when snapped by a signalman's son, who himself became a railwayman. This handsome loco also survived the war and entered BR stock in 1948, but the entire class was scrapped by 1951

D. Fereday Glenn collection, courtesy of Mr L. Goff

In immaculate olive green livery, fully lined-out, class I3 4-4-2T No. 2082 posed for the photographer outside Littlehampton shed in the mid-thirties. This type of engine handled much of the passenger traffic along the coast between Brighton and Portsmouth before electrification, and most found other more local duties until the early years of BR. The last of the class was scrapped in 1952

D. Fereday Glenn collection, courtesy Mr L. Goff

The last of these fine shed scenes of Littlehampton in the 1930s shows a former LSWR visitor. Class S11 4-4-0 No. 395 was the first of ten engines with 6 ft driving wheels – which were based on Drummond's earlier T9 design and intended for passenger duties on more steeply graded routes west of Salisbury. The distinctive 'Watercart' bogie tender can clearly be seen. No. 395 survived until 1951

D. Fereday Glenn collection, courtesy Mr L. Goff

Part 2 : Westwards from Woking

The rebuilt 'Battle of Britain' Pacific No. 34087 *145 Squadron* carefully negotiates newly relaid track on the quadruple main line between Woking and Basingstoke with a Waterloo to Weymouth express on 13.11.65. The electric third-rail is already in position but not energized while work continues on both up and down fast lines, in preparation for full multiple unit operation in mid-1967

Travelling just a little too fast for the photographer's camera, a rebuilt 'Merchant Navy' 4-6-2 No. 35010 *Blue Star* hauls the down 'Bournemouth Belle' Pullman (the 12.30 p.m. departure from London, Waterloo) near Brookwood on 19.5.66. The track at this point had been completely prepared for electric operation on all four lines, and it was to be the last year that steam haulage of the 'Belle' could be relied upon. The Pullman brake immediately behind the engine was also nearing the end of its working life, to be replaced by a suitably painted standard 'BG' full brake van for the final season of this famous train

The last surviving Peppercorn Pacific, class A2 No. 60532 *Blue Peter*, was much in demand for rail tours in the mid-sixties. On 14.8.66 it had charge of an enthusiasts' special from Waterloo to Exeter. In pleasant weather conditions *Blue Peter* headed down the four-track section near the site of the abandoned Bramshot Halt (closed in May 1946) between Farnborough and Fleet. In the background a gantry spans the line, bereft of all its semaphore signal arms, while the third rail is now in place

Under a lowering sky, rebuilt 'Merchant Navy' 4-6-2 No. 35023 thunders through Brookwood with an up Weymouth express, despite being routed on the 'slow' line. The reason for this was that an up express from Exeter was on the 'fast' line, but the photographer's wish to get the two trains running neck-and-neck was frustrated by *Holland-Afrika Line* accelerating ahead. This picture was taken on 3.6.67, just five weeks before the end of steam

A down freight headed by a Standard 5MT 4-6-0 No. 73082 (formerly *Camelot*) moves along the slow line above the A321 main road west of Brookwood, 19.5.66. Happily No. 73082 has been retrieved from Barry scrapyard and is being restored to full working order at the Bluebell Railway for the 1990s

In appalling weather, Woking station echoed to the sound of a Gresley on 26.3.66 when class A4 Pacific No. 60024 *Kingfisher* swept through at high speed on a Waterloo to Weymouth special. Formerly at Edinburgh Haymarket, the engine was then used on the Glasgow to Aberdeen expresses in the mid-1960s. *Kingfisher* was a popular engine that did not find a home in preservation – the weekend it spent on the Southern in March 1966 was a poignant farewell

Despite the branch being closed for fourteen years, the station nameboard still showed 'Brookwood for Bisley Camp' on 10.9.66. The Bulleid 'West County' Pacific No. 34023 *Blackmore Vale* maintained the old Southern tradition with a lengthy train of green carriages forming a down express from Waterloo to Bournemouth and Weymouth. This engine was never sent for scrap: after a period of preservation at Longmoor, it is now kept on the Bluebell Railway

Only one example of the small class of 3MT 2-6-0 Standard engines ever came south; having been borrowed for a rail tour it stayed to the end of steam. No. 77014, in unlined black livery, is seen here at Woking station on Sunday, 14.8.66, perhaps helping out on engineers' trains. In the last few years of steam traction, much engineering work was needed to allow all services to be worked by diesel or electric traction only, thereby making more work for the very motive power it was intended to make redundant

Standard 4MT 2-6-0 No. 76069 trundled through Woking station with an engineers' train for the yard on Sunday, 14.8.66. The bogie Bolster wagons were (and still are) used for track panels, while next to the engine was one of the distinctive 'Shark' plough brake vans often used in reballasting work. Behind stands one of the brand new electro-diesel locomotives, No. E6034, painted in an attractive shade of blue with white roof. More than twenty years on, that same electro-diesel is numbered 73.127 and takes its turn on the Gatwick Express and other passenger duties

Part 3 : Suburban Splendour

Contrasts in adjoining platforms at Surbiton on 2.12.62. While the combined Alton and Portsmouth stopping service from Waterloo was provided, as usual, by a rake of two-car electric multiple units (2-HAL No. 2648 leading), a rail tour to Hampton Court was hauled by a brace of Beattie well-tanks. Dating back to 1874, 0298 class 2-4-0WTs Nos. 30585 and 30587, have been meticulously prepared for their swansong, having been banished from the London area before the turn of the century. Both have been preserved as examples of Victorian steam power

Another contrast to be seen at Surbiton on 2.12.62 was this aged – but still working – coal lorry. Built not far away at Guildford by Dennis Brothers in 1930, the elderly vehicle was largely original with oval side- and rear-view windows, miniature side lights and solitary headlight. The battered front wings bear witness to a long and arduous working life, while the faded paintwork informs us that the firm of W. Crocker had been established in 1898

A crisp December morning helped to ensure a dramatic steam and smoke effect from two octogenarian locomotives as they wait for the 'off' alongside the platform at Surbiton. Numbered 3314 and 3298 respectively before nationalization, 2-4-0WTs Nos. 30585/30587 look to be in pristine condition for their outing to Hampton Court on 2.12.62. The rail tour was so popular that it had to be repeated a fortnight later

Darkening the sky with their combined exhausts, Beattie well-tanks Nos. 30585 and 30587 make a suitably sedate exit from Surbiton on 2.12.62. heading for Hampton Court with the first of two rail tours of surburban lines from which they had been exiled more than sixty years earlier. Both engines survive today and No. 30585 (restored as Southern Railway 0314) has been steamed again at Quainton Road in Buckinghamshire

To simplify watering, and running-round, well-tank No. 30585 was uncoupled from its twin at Hampton Court station, 2.12.62. The miniscule bunker and small water capacity can be seen clearly in this close-up view at the historic terminus, although the eighty-eight-year-old engine did not seem to have any difficulty in producing plentiful supplies of steam. Note the tapered-off electric third-rail short of the buffer-stops

It was difficult to photograph the veteran pair upon arrival at Hampton Court because of the brilliant sunshine and the crowds of well-wishers. There was an added problem – refilling the well-tanks with water. Class 0298 2-4-0WTs Nos. 30585/30587 are standing at the platform where they were admired by vast numbers of enthusiasts on 2.12.62

The idea of running the last active examples of erstwhile South Western suburban tank engines on their original routes before they were withdrawn inspired several interesting rail tours in the early 1960s. On 19.3.61, one of the Adams 'Radial' 4-4-2T engines that had been the mainstay of the Axminster to Lyme Regis line for nearly half a century left Waterloo for a tour of London outer suburban routes. With a suitable 'period' train of three non-corridor carriages, class 0415 No. 30582 (formerly Southern Railway No. 3125) paused at Chertsey for a photographic stop on a fine spring afternoon. Fellow 'Radial' tank No. 30583 was purchased later the same year for active preservation on the Bluebell Railway

J. Courtney Haydon

Although many examples of the small-wheeled 02 class 0-4-4T remained in use on the Isle of Wight, by the sixties only a handful were left on the mainland. One of the last was No. 30199 (previously based at Wadebridge in Cornwall) which headed a rail tour from Waterloo on 25.3.62. During a circuit of the Kingston loop, No. 30199 was spotted coasting into Twickenham to take water before continuing on to Norwood Junction. On this occasion three non-corridor coaches had been borrowed from the London Midland Region as they were suitable for use on certain London Transport tracks; the Southern had none left by this time

28

Urie's career on the LSWR was crowned with two magnificent large tank engine designs. The first of these was a class of four 4-8-0T locos for hump shunting at Feltham marshalling yard, introduced in 1921. With the arrival of diesel shunters there was no longer a need for such massive steam engines: two were taken out of service in 1959, but the other pair were kept busy on transfer freights across London. On 5.11.60 class G16 No. 30494 created its own kind of fireworks display as it set in motion a long train of fitted wagons bound for Willesden, a veritable Goliath of a machine

Urie's other large tank design called for five 4-6-2T locomotives, which entered service in 1921/2 as class H16. These rugged machines spent most of their forty years working transfer freights across London, although they had a short spell on the Eastleigh to Fawley oil-tank trains in 1960/1. The last survivor, No. 30517, worked a rail tour to Chessington on 2.12.62 (having taken over from the Beattie well-tanks after their visit to Hampton Court earlier in the day). It is seen here passing Chessington North in fine style

The suburban rail tour proved so popular that a repeat performance was staged two weeks later. On 16.12.62 the immaculate 'H16' again took a six-coach train along the electrified branch to Chessington South, giving photographers a fresh excuse to expend film on a handsome locomotive which, sadly, was not preserved. In this view the distinctive shape of the canopies at Chessington North station can be seen in the background, while No. 30517 eases the lightweight 200-ton train for Chessington South. While passenger trains terminate here, the track continues to a coal concentration depot further on

As the short winters day ends, class H16 4-6-2T No. 30517 gives tongue while crossing over from the down to the up line on leaving Chessington South station on 16.12.62. This rail tour marked the farewell of the last Pacific tank engine in Britain; all remaining G16 and H16 tanks were withdrawn by the end of the year

Part 4 : Outer Suburbia

On the border between Surrey and Hampshire, near Froyle, class S15 4-6-0 No. 30837 crosses the River Wey with a rail tour bound for the coast via the mid-Hants line on 16.1.66. This was another repeat excursion, but there had been no snow for the trip the previous week

For the Portsmouth and Alton electrification scheme, electric multiple units on stopping services split up or joined at Woking. The carriage sheds for Alton line services were built at Farnham, but freight traffic continued to rely on steam power. On 14.11.66 one of the Standard 4MT 2-6-0s formerly allocated to the Midland & Great Northern routes in East Anglia (note the cut-away section below the cab, for automatic collection of single-line tablet), No. 76033, trundled along tender-first through Alice Holt woods between Farnham and Bentley with goods wagons for Alton yard

The electrified track ended at Alton, although the connection via Alresford to Winchester (City) was maintained by diesel multiple units until 1973, when it was closed. On 16.1.66 class S15 4-6-0 No. 30837 waits by the up main platform at Alton in arctic conditions while the rail tour travelled over the Bentley to Bordon branch. Note the gas and electric lighting in use here

Part 5 : Cross-Country Between Reading and Redhill

On the border between Surrey and Berkshire a late afternoon train from Redhill to Reading (South) clatters along amid rural surroundings near Crowthorne on 11.8.58. Class U 2-6-0 No. 31799 makes light work of its four-coach load, which consists of a 'narrow' set of corridor stock (set 452) used on former SECR routes with restricted clearances. This locomotive was one of those rebuilt from 'River' class 2-6-4Ts

In the opposite direction Standard class 4MT 2-6-0 No. 76053 is in charge of a Reading (South) to Redhill train between Wokingham and Crowthorne where the route passes beneath Nine Mile Ride, 11.8.58. Three- or four-coach trains were the usual load in steam days with 'Mogul' 2-6-0s being ideal motive power

Typical of the lengthy goods trains that used to travel over the Reading to Redhill line, Class N 2-6-0 No. 31864 eases through Guildford under light steam having come down the hill from Wanborough, 26.5.63. The first vehicle in the train is a new maroon-liveried bogie GUV van. Being a Sunday, the storage siding just north of the central platforms did not contain spare electric multiple unit stock, so the photographer's view was completely uncluttered. Note the old signalbox behind the tender of the engine

For many years 4-4-0s of both LSWR and SECR parentage were to be found at work on the Reading to Redhill cross-country line. From the 1950s onwards 'Schools' class locomotives made an occasional appearance. On 4.7.60 three-cylinder V No. 30906 *Sherborne* pulled into platform 5 at Guildford with a three-coach load for Redhill. The Maunsell carriage on the right of the picture formed part of a push–pull set used on the branch line to Horsham, converted earlier the same year to replace elderly non-corridor pre-grouping stock

One train daily between Reading and Redhill brought a Western Region engine on to the line. Seen here is 43xx 2-6-0 No. 5368 exhibiting a GWR headlamp code (single lamp below the chimney) when working a Redhill to Reading service on 23.11.57. The train, which consisted of flat-sided Maunsell stock for former SECR restricted routes, was photographed as it ran into Guildford with a good head of steam. The depot (70C) and turntable for the roundhouse were on a cramped site adjoining the track at this point

Here the 6.16 p.m. train to Dorking Town is waiting to leave Guildford, 4.7.60. One of the Bulleid 'Austerity' Q1 0-6-0s that had been based at 70C for many years, No. 33005, has been pressed into passenger service and obscures much of the old station building as the driver opens the regulator. Note the twin water columns on platforms 4 and 5, with the train of 2-HAL electric units on a service to Aldershot and Waterloo via Ash Vale and Virginia Water

One or two of the 'Coppertop' Wainwright D class 4-4-0s could be found taking their turn on local passenger duties between Reading and Redhill until 1956. On 2.9.55 No. 31075 and 'period' train of SECR 'Birdcage' carriages formed such a service, with the old 4-4-0 emitting steam as it restarted from platform 5 at Guildford on its journey eastward. The screen between the coaling stage and platform 8 can be seen on the left; both it and the canopied buildings have since been demolished during the rebuilding of the Guildford station complex

A double-headed freight for the Redhill line leaves Guildford on 23.11.57 with tender-first class 700 No. 30693 leading Q class No. 30549 under the Farnham Road bridge. Both 0-6-0s carry headcode discs, but the crew must have found it cold on a raw November day driving their old 'Black Motor' backwards into an easterly wind

Later, class 700 0-6-0 No. 30693 brings back a short pick-up goods from Dorking past the engine shed and turntable at Guildford on 23.11.57. This engine, already sixty years old, spent some years based at 70C; it occasionally worked the Petersfield to Midhurst goods in the period 1948–51

A much heavier freight train for Redhill yard on 23.11.57 called for something bigger than a mere 0-6-0. Class S15 4-6-0 No. 30835 opens up to some effect with a load of coal wagons as it passes Guildford shed on its way to the tunnel and Shalford Junction. This engine was one of five S15s equipped with six-wheel tenders for the shorter turntables found on central and eastern sections of the Southern

By no means common on the cross-country route, Standard class 4MT 2-6-4T No. 80032 leaves a trail of steam and smoke as it pulls away from Guildford with a Reading (South) to Redhill passenger train, 23.11.57. This Standard tank exhibits a 75A (Brighton) shed plate, and may have been borrowed by Redhill to cover a temporary shortage of motive power. Note the flat-sided Maunsell corridor set 184 in tow

In a rarely photographed location between Guildford's two tunnels, class V 4-4-0 No. 30917 *Ardingly* speeds the 2.50 p.m. Reading South to Redhill train along as the autumn light begins to fade on 26.10.61. Half the 'Schools' class were equipped by Bulleid with large diameter double chimneys, but it seemed to make no difference to their performance one way or the other

A frosty winter's day accentuates the trail of smoke and steam produced by class S15 4-6-0 No. 30835 with a Redhill-bound freight, 7.12.61. The train has just crossed the River Wey between Shalford Junction and Shalford station, where there was once a spur line connecting southward with the Portsmouth Direct route (avoiding Guildford)

With safety valves blowing off, class U 2-6-0 No. 31628 proceeds cautiously after leaving Shalford station as the distant signal warns that the junction is not clear. Although only midday, the hazy winter sunshine creates a dramatic shadow of the engine in the shallow cutting on 12.12.61, as No. 31628 heads west with a Redhill to Reading freight

The sharpness of the curve from Shalford Junction can be appreciated in this view of class S15 4-6-0 No. 30847 with a Redhill freight, 12.12.61. This was Maunsell's last 4-6-0: built with an eight-wheel bogie tender, it acquired a central section six-wheel variety in its final years, perhaps from a withdrawn engine, to work on this cross-country route. After spending some years in Barry scrapyard, the locomotive is now being restored to working order on the Bluebell Railway with the correct pattern bogie tender

A green-liveried Western Region 2-6-0 in the shape of 'Mogul' No. 7331 steams away from Shalford with the characteristic sharp exhaust note on 12.12.61 at the head of a Redhill to Reading local train. The stock comprises a set of Standard Mk 1 carriages (540) while the engine is one of the series with side-window cabs, formerly numbered in the 93xx batch

By 1964 steam operations on the Southern's Reading to Redhill line were fairly run down, both locomotives and rolling stock being at a low ebb. To economize on passenger facilities as an alternative to complete withdrawal, a curious diesel train was put together. It consisted of two early Hastings line carriages (including a driving motor brake) coupled to a non-corridor driving trailer from a surplus suburban electric unit. The resulting three-coach set was nicknamed a 'Tadpole' unit due to its odd shape – two flat-sided short corridor carriages next to a normal width, standard length non-corridor driving trailer – altogether six were assembled. Being fitted with a 500 bhp engine instead of the 600 bhp type used in Hampshire or Sussex diesel units, the 'Tadpoles' were rather underpowered. Given the TOPS coding 206, what was essentially a stop-gap measure provided a local service – of sorts – on the Reading to Redhill and Tonbridge line for fifteen years, although they were never popular and became increasingly unreliable with the passage of time. With headcode 88, unit 1206 is recorded on 24.5.65 as it leaves Shalford on route for Reading

With a dusting of snow where the sun has not yet penetrated, class Q1 0-6-0 No. 33025 bustles out of Shalford with the 9.45 a.m. Reading to Redhill service on 7.12.61. The use of such an engine on passenger trains was probably not envisaged by Mr Bulleid when he designed his 'Austerity' class in the dark days of 1942 but it was fairly commonplace, both from Guildford and Eastleigh depots

A more familiar task for a Q1 was the haulage of heavy freight, such as this loaded ballast train bound for Redhill. 0-6-0 No. 33036 thunders through Gomshall & Shere station during the morning of 10.1.62 with a 'plough' brake van next to the tender. Forty of these ugly engines were constructed: intended for a life of just ten years, most were still at work after twenty. The original C1 (No. 33001) has been saved for the National Collection and can be seen at Sheffield Park station on the Bluebell Railway

With the gradient rising to 1 in 96 through Gomshall & Shere, class N 2-6-0 No. 31872 is obliged to work hard at the head of a very mixed goods from Reading to Redhill, 10.1.62. Note the modern flat-bottomed track nearest the camera but with the traditional bull-head type still in use for eastbound trains

Clean but bereft of nameplates, 'Battle of Britain' 4-6-2 No. 34087 (formerly *145 Squadron*) hustles a rail tour along between Betchworth and Dorking on its way to Guildford, 5.3.67. Despite the overcast weather, the rebuilt Pacific manages to leave a clear trail of smoke and steam to mark its passage, running parallel to the A25 main road at this point. This special provided the last (and only) chance for a photograph here before the end of steam traction on the Southern

A last glimpse of an older generation of passenger locomotive built for the SECR. With no frills or unnecessary ornamentation, Borsig of Germany manufactured some of the Wainwright designed L class 4-4-0s, including No. 31771, here seen at Redhill on 12.5.57. The 74D shedcode indicates this engine had been prepared for working back home to Tonbridge. A few of these handsome engines were painted malachite green following the cessation of hostilities in 1945; after nationalization, the words 'British Railways' were substituted for Southern on the tender, but the colourful livery was retained as long as possible

After the grouping, Maunsell brought out a further series of inside cylinder 4-4-0s, designated class L1, in 1926. These engines had side-window cabs but with raised frames over the coupling rods, like the rebuilt D1 and E1 classes. No. 31785 is awaiting a fresh spell of activity at Redhill, 3.3.57

Part 6 : The 'New Line' to Guildford

The 'new line' from Surbiton to Guildford via Effingham Junction was opened in 1885, running first through outer suburbia and then 'stock broker belt' country to provide a useful alternative to the main route via Woking. While, today, it may be operated by the most modern type of third-rail electric suburban units, in 1961 it was not uncommon to find services maintained by quite elderly stock. Built in 1925 as a three-car unit, 4-SUB No. 4333 had been strengthened by the addition of a modern steel-bodied trailer seating six-a-side in ten compartments – 120 extra passengers in the rush hour. With the original stencilled headcode 'H' in position, unit 4333 performs a routine mid-morning journey from Guildford to Waterloo via Effingham Junction and the Cobham line on 11.10.61, leaving Clandon station long after the commuters have gone to work

Much more typical of the Leatherhead–Guildford goods in 1961 was the use of a 'Vulcan' C2x 0-6-0. On 13 October No. 32547 trundled through Clandon with a solitary wagon and brake van in tow, though a couple of engineers' wagons have somehow appeared in the goods yard overnight. The double-slip in the trackwork should be noted here

With some commuters' cars to be seen in the deserted goods yard, Drummond class 700 0-6-0 No. 30326 returns home to Guildford from an unaccustomed foray on the 11.10 a.m. goods from Leatherhead, seen passing Clandon on 12.10.61. Though scheduled to operate on weekdays, Saturday excepted, it was not unknown at this time for the freight to run on Monday, Wednesday and Friday only (MWFO). It was generally the preserve of a Norwood Junction engine, whereas the sixty-four-year-old 'Black Motor' had been based at Guildford for years; the author first came across it on Petersfield to Midhurst goods duties in 1948

The days of the 'Vulcan' were numbered, for on 5.12.61 the 11.10 a.m. Leatherhead goods was headed by three-cylinder class U1 2-6-0 No. 31903. The newly-affixed 75C shedplate shows up clearly on the smokebox door as No. 31903 rattles through Clandon at a fair pace. These freight trains were the only regular excuse for steam power on this electrified line

On a damp autumn morning, class C2x 0-6-0 No. 32547 brings a load of coal wagons through London Road station, 20.10.61. At this time of year the 11.10 a.m. freight from Leatherhead to Guildford might be expected to convey a few of these wagons. Note the covered lattice footbridge and lack of any passengers at this time of day. The 'Vulcan' has a 73A shedplate

With part of the engine showing some sign of attention from the cleaners, class U1 2-6-0 No. 31896 leans to the curve on leaving London Road station before sweeping round in the opposite direction into Guildford itself on 21.11.61. London Road goods siding has some coal wagons in residence

With safety valves lifting obligingly, 'Battle of Britain' 4-6-2 No. 34052 (formerly *Lord Dowding*) sweeps through London Road in charge of a rail tour to Southampton, Andover and the Ludgershall branch, 9.10.66. Steam-hauled passenger trains were a rarity on this line and brought out photographers in their droves. Semaphore signals have given way to modern colour lights, although the sighting panel remains starkly white on the bridge behind

Class U1 'Mogul' 31900 appears out of the shadows at London Road station with the 11.10 a.m. Leatherhead to Guildford goods, 2.11.61. Note the platform starting home signal, with co-acting arms and sighting panel painted on the bridge behind. No headcode discs and just a single lamp are in evidence on the engine

Presenting a strange spectacle at the head of a passenger train, class 0395 0-6-0 No. 30567 looms out of the mist with the Portsmouth Direct Line Centenarian rail tour on Sunday, 25.1.59. One of the last survivors of the 1881 Adams design, No. 30567 had been reboilered with a former London, Chatham & Dover pattern from a small 4-4-0. This veteran was photographed between London Road and Guildford stations on the embankment just above the River Wey; its train included some Pullman cars, and must have been a very unusual sight over the electrified 'new line' at any time. No. 30567 had been built in 1883 by Neilson

Possibly the last occasion a 'Vulcan' worked the 11.10 a.m. Leatherhead to Guildford goods, class C2x No. 32521 of Norwood Junction shed was commendably clean and carried a most unusual headlamp code, 16.11.61. The pick-up goods was an ideal task for this sort of engine, which had an assortment of mineral wagons as its load on this date. This particular 0-6-0 was often rostered to work the Pulborough–Midhurst–Petersfield branch freight during the 1951–4 period when based at Horsham depot.

Part 7 : Guildford Station Scenes

Taking water at the top end of the yard furthest from the shed, the unique 'Q' 0-6-0 No. 30549 shows off its stovepipe chimney in the winter sunlight, 23.11.57. Some cattle vans and a traditional Southern brake can be seen against the background of the houses

The last of the famous D class 4-4-0s, No. 31737 was retained for light duties at Guildford in 1956. Pictured near the coaling stage on 11 August of that year, a 2-BIL electric unit on the Aldershot service, and covered footbridge to Park Road can also be seen. No. 31737 was preserved for the National Collection, and can be seen in York Museum restored to the ornate livery of the South Eastern & Chatham Railway

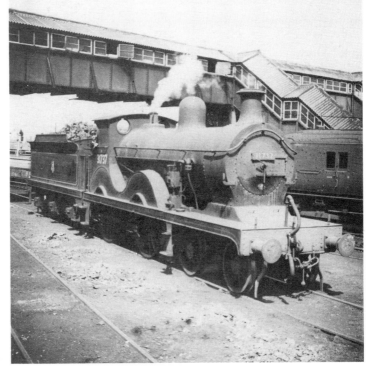

Built by Dubs of Glasgow in 1897, class 700 0-6-0 No. 30339 was nearing the end of a long career when pictured running light past the turntable at Guildford on 5.2.62. The last Drummond 'Black Motor' was withdrawn in 1963; regrettably, none were preserved

Farewell to a Victorian veteran: suitably decorated with a headboard to commemorate the opening of the Portsmouth Direct railway from Farncombe to Havant in 1859, Adams '0395' 0-6-0 No. 30567 takes a breather at Guildford after bringing in its special train, 25.1.59. Numbered 3154 in Southern Railway days, this was one of the last duties performed by this locomotive before withdrawal. It ended its days at Feltham (70B) depot

Looking spotless near the coaling stage on 23.11.57, class E4 0-6-2T No. 32505 was a Guildford engine suitable for mixed traffic duties, most probably on the Horsham branch. Fortunately, one of these has been saved for the Bluebell Railway and, as *Birch Grove*, No. 473 can be seen in its proper environment

Though far from perfect technically, this picture has been included as it proved to be the author's only photographic record of Drummond's last (arguably, his finest) express 4-4-0 design. Class D15 No. 30465 was also the sole survivor of the ten examples of this type by 2.9.55. After coming off shed, the engine ran behind the coaling screen at Guildford, thus eluding the camera; this picture was taken from a Waterloo-bound train as it overtook the D15 near where the Aldershot and Reading line diverges from the main line. No. 30465 was withdrawn four months later and none of this type were preserved. These engines had worked the Portsmouth to Bristol inter-regional trains before the introduction of BR Standard 4MT 2-6-0s in 1952

Perhaps because of their greater numbers, Drummond's 'T9' design outlived the larger D15 by several years. On 17.4.59 'Greyhound' No. 30732 was in light steam near the coaling stage at Guildford, overshadowed by the extended footbridge to Park Road. Note the huge 'Watercart' bogie tender with which many T9 class 4-4-0s were fitted, enabling them to run prodigious distances on a single tenderful of coal and water

Part 8 : The Guildford–Horsham Branch

Puffing vigorously at the rear, class M7 0-4-4T No. 30047 propels an old LSWR corridor push–pull set (strengthened by the addition of a former SECR ten-compartment non-corridor bogie) out of Guildford, beneath the Farnham Road bridge towards Horsham on 23.11.57. Most of the steam heating seems to be under the boiler rather than under the carriages

With the frost lingering on the sleepers of the single line, Ivatt 2MT 2-6-2T No. 41287 speeds along in fine style between Peasmarsh Junction and the first station at Bramley & Wonersh with the 10.34 a.m. Guildford to Horsham branch train, 7.12.61. On the right of the picture is the abandoned stump of the Wey and Arun Canal, obscured by all the vegetation

With the early morning mist clearing slowly, an unusual working brought class Q1 0-6-0 No. 33019 and the Guildford breakdown crane to the Horsham branch at Peasmarsh Junction, 22.11.61. Today the former trackbed is completely overgrown at this point

Though only a couple of miles from Guildford, this view of the Horsham pick-up goods gives every appearance of being 'far from the madding crowd'. On 19.2.62 class M7 0-4-4T No. 30132 trundles, bunker-first, along the straight stretch of track between Bramley & Wonersh station and the junction with the Porstmouth line at Peasmarsh, parallel with the forgotten remains of the Wey and Arun Canal

Class 2MT 2-6-2T No. 41261 brings the 10.34 a.m. Guildford to Horsham branch train under the Cranleigh road bridge near Smithwood Common on 6.12.61. These 'Mickey Mouse' tanks had a fair turn of speed and were ideal little engines for this sort of traffic. By this date the branch train consisted of a Bulleid three-coach 'shortie' set, but the mid-morning train was not heavily patronized

The thrice-weekly branch goods generally needed to shunt in the yard at Cranleigh, probably the busiest station on the line. On 6.12.61 M7 No. 30378 had left its train in the down platform and was in the process of running round when pictured passing this interesting 'shunt' arm signal. The entire site of Cranleigh station has been redeveloped and is unrecognizable today

Horsham depot turned out an old Brighton 'Radial' for the 3.09 p.m. branch train to Guildford on 16.6.61. The class E4 0-6-2T, No. 32469, recalled the charm of this Sussex/Surrey byway as it left Cranleigh bunker first with push–pull set 614. None of the E4 tanks was equipped with motor-train fittings, so it had to run round the carriages at each terminus

Class M7 0-4-4T No. 30132 steams along at a good pace with the Horsham branch goods between Cranleigh and Baynards on 7.2.62. The fifty-nine-year-old Drummond tank has been given some attention by the cleaners at 70C and looks very smart, even if it is heading a freight train rather than the passenger traffic for which it was designed. No. 30132 was withdrawn nine months later, but two examples of the M7 have been preserved

The usual 'M7' tank must have been unavailable on 15.1.62, as the Horsham branch freight was in the care of a Bulleid class Q1 0-6-0. With four mineral wagons and a goods brake, No. 33025 was super-power indeed for such a train as it shuffles away from Cranleigh towards Baynards

A delightful scene at Baynards station on 16.6.61. The crew have left the up branch goods in the platform while they enjoy a cup of tea, but the signal is pulled off ready for imminent departure towards Guildford. Bunker first M7 0-4-4T No. 30378 shows a wisp of steam from its safety valves, in readiness for some hard work ahead with this lengthy train. The goods shed is empty, save for the platelayer's trolley, but the 1930s car seems entirely appropriate

After leaving Baynards, the branch freight heads across the border into Sussex and the yard at Rudgwick station. One of the regular branch engines, No. 30132, leaves a trail of frothy white smoke and steam as it thunders beneath the skew bridge and gathers pace before the tunnel, bound for Horsham on 14.2.62

Last train: two of the remaining Q1s, Nos. 33027 and 33006, were allotted the sad task of bringing the final rail tour from Horsham to Guildford on 13.6.65. As the light was fading, the pair of wartime 0-6-0s got to grips with the lengthy train as they passed through Christ's Hospital on their way home. Another branch line passed into history

Part 9 : From Horsham to the Coast

Alongside, but separate from, the former Guildford branch platforms at Christ's Hospital are those for trains from Horsham to the coast. Until March 1966 they were also used by non-electrified services between Horsham, Shoreham and Brighton. On 19.2.62 the gloomy winter weather was relieved by one of the Brighton-based 'Mickey Mouse' 2MT 2-6-2T locomotives (No. 41300) noisily restarting a Horsham train from the up electrified platform

A Horsham to Brighton service was maintained even on Sundays. The newly converted push–pull set 604 formed the 5.19 p.m. from Horsham and is being propelled away from Christ's Hospital on 24.4.60 by one of the old Drummond 'M7' 0-4-4Ts, No. 30051. The Maunsell corridor stock was strengthened by the addition of a SECR ten-compartment non-corridor carriage next to the engine, which had been transferred to 75D in the early 1950s for push–pull services to Midhurst and Petersfield, as well as duties to Shoreham and Brighton

The up branch goods from Shoreham to Horsham passes Itchingfield Junction 'box on 19.2.62 as it approaches Christ's Hospital (West Horsham). After the withdrawal of the last of the LBSCR 'Vulcan' 0-6-0s the previous month, class Q No. 30547 was used to help out, having been fitted with a single blastpipe chimney of the usual BR pattern in place of its Bulleid double blastpipe variety. Note the antique track maintenance vehicle in the down yard

Very little steam power was seen on the Arun Valley (mid-Sussex) line after withdrawal of passenger trains between Pulborough, Midhurst and Petersfield in February 1955. Goods traffic was maintained as far as Midhurst until 1964, but this became increasingly seasonal so that trains might run only two or three days per week. However, class E4 0-6-2T No. 32470 is here performing with great gusto between Pulborough and Billingshurst on 14.3.62, heading a mixed load that included a couple of grain wagons from the Midhurst branch

Tank engines usually worked chimney first to Horsham and returned to Brighton bunker first. One fine day in September 1963 a very scruffy 'Mickey Mouse' 2MT 2-6-2T (believed to be No. 41326) was in charge of the 12.19 p.m. from Horsham when it paused at the deserted Southwater station. By this stage the line was in decline: because it was double track throughout, signalling had been dispensed with here and the goods yard was disused. In contrast to previous years, the rolling stock was unkempt: the end was in sight – it closed in March 1966, despite dieselization

In happier days, a Horsham to Brighton local service might produce an engine of rare quality. On 23.4.50 a morning train to the coast comprised an ex-LBSCR push–pull set, freshly painted in BR crimson livery, with an I3 4-4-2T at the front. Although No. 32088 was carrying its BR number on the bunker sides, no smokebox numberplate had been fitted and the tank sides still bore the legend 'Southern' in faded 'sunshine' lettering. This was pictured at West Grinstead station, 45¼ miles from London

R.C. Riley

By drafting in ex-LSWR 0-4-4T engines to replace the vanishing LBSCR designs, shortages of suitable push–pull locomotives were made good during the early 1950s. Drummond M7 No. 30053 shuffles away from Partridge Green station with a motor train of arc-roofed carriages towards Horsham on 23.6.56. This locomotive escaped the scrap merchant, was exported to America and has since returned to Britain for a fresh lease of life on the Swanage Railway in the 1990s

R.C. Riley

The late afternoon sunshine, shows class E5x 0-6-2T No. 2576 (renumbered No. 32576 after nationalization) ready to depart from Brightons's imposing terminal with a local service for Horsham, 29.6.46. Shaded 'sunshine' lettering introduced by Bulleid relieves the plain black paintwork, while first and third class seating is available. Rebuilding four of the E5 'Radials' with C3 boilers gave them a more modern shape

R.C. Riley

Part 10 : Coastway West from Brighton

A passenger on a train leaving Brighton for Worthing, Littlehampton, Chichester or Portsmouth might have been amused to see the quaint little P 0-6-0T on the coal wagons that largely obscured the shed from view. On 9.6.57 a very respectable No. 31556 was in charge, having been given a good clean beforehand. Eight of these small engines were built by the SECR for light passenger duties in the late Edwardian period, but ended their days shunting; four have been preserved

For many years the old station at Chichester had been something of a disgrace, aggravated by numerous level-crossings nearby. By 1963, although the station had been dramatically rebuilt, the problem with road intersections remained (as it does to this day). On 3.11.63 a last special train was run to say farewell to the Hayling Island branch – home for seventy years to numbers of Stroudley 'Terriers' – and also to visit what remained of the Chichester to Midhurst line. Two of the dwindling Q class 0-6-0s were roped in to take the rail tour to and from Lavant and then back to London. As the sun was setting, No. 30531 (with double chimney) and No. 30543 (with BR Standard chimney) made ready in the fading light for their long journey

One of the more ambitious rail tours of the 1960s took in visits to a number of Sussex branch lines as well as a trip along the coastal route (the Coastway West title was not bestowed until the seventies). On 24.6.62 class K 2-6-0 No. 32353 was steaming along in superb fashion as it passed Barnham Junction heading west in the early afternoon

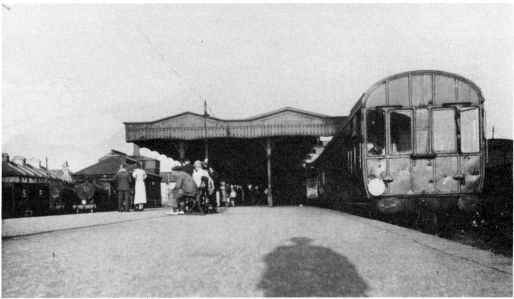

Before electrification of the coastal line, local services to and from Littlehampton were provided by a steam-hauled push–pull train which connected with the main route at Ford. This thirties view of Littlehampton shows the driving end of the 'Balloon' push–pull set No. 739 while, on the far left, two 4-4-0s from the former rival constituents of the Southern Railway can be seen. The LBSCR engine is a B4, the LSWR version being most likely a S11 or a L12. Note the fashions of passengers standing in front of the small engine shed

D. Fereday Glenn collection, courtesy Mr L. Goff

One of the most unusual visitors in the final days of steam was Lord Garnock's preserved Gresley three-cylinder K4 2-6-0 *The Great Marquess*. Built for the West Highland route to Fort William and Mallaig in Scotland, it was restored to the LNER apple green livery and numbered 3442 in the early 1960s – its BR number had been 61994. On 12.3.67 it made its only pilgrimage to the far south, the smart green paintwork brightening an otherwise gloomy day as it charged along the 6-mile straight track between Barnham Junction and Chichester on its way to Southampton

Passenger traffic between Chichester and Midhurst had been withdrawn in 1935, but freight continued to use the single track until a landslip occurred north of Cocking and derailed the pick-up goods to Midhurst on 19.11.51. After a short period of operation between Chichester and Cocking, it was cut back to Lavant only – which thus became the railhead for a considerable sugar-beet traffic until the end of steam. On 19.5.61 class Q1 0-6-0 No. 33021 was returning to Chichester with just a couple of empty wagons and brake van in the shallow cutting amid open fields north of Brandy Hole Lane

With the afternoon sun hidden by the depth of the cutting, two Q 0-6-0s (No. 30543 leading No. 30531) bring a rail tour into Lavant on 3.11.63. Not since the royal trains to Singleton for the Goodwood Races had such an impressive special been seen on the Chichester to Midhurst branch

Some evidence of the gracious architecture to be found at LBSCR railway stations still prevailed at Lavant, even though passenger services had been suspended for more than twenty years. On 1.7.59, class E4 0-6-2T No. 32495 provided the authentic Brighton image after shunting the yard, waiting to return to Chichester with the pick-up goods. The details of this scene deserve study, for they embody much of the atmosphere of a working railway that so appeals to observers of the steam age. The canopy of Lavant station has been dismantled and taken to the Bluebell Railway, where it will be re-erected one day at Horsted Keynes

Too long for the limited station facilities at Lavant, the rail tour on 3.10.65 had a Q1 0-6-0 at either end of the train. Wagons loaded with sugar beet stand in the yard beside No. 33027 at the Midhurst end of the special, while No. 33020 faces towards Chichester at the other end of the carriages. Only a handful of these ugly machines remained in traffic by this time, but they were much in demand for rail tours. The first to be built, C1 (No. 33001), has been saved for the National Collection

A happy event in 1961 was the delivery – in steam, by rail – of the Bluebell Railway's latest acquisition: the former LSWR 4-4-2T No. 488 was the last survivor of the famous Adams 'Radial' tanks so long associated with the Lyme Regis branch and seen here under its own power. It was a long journey for such an elderly engine and frequent stops had to be planned to replenish its modest water supply. With its BR number (No. 30583) painted out, the veteran of 1885 continued its eastbound journey between Havant and Chichester, passing Warblington Halt on the afternoon of 9.7.61

Steam and snow are an irresistable combination. In smart Brunswick green paintwork, 'Schools' class 4-4-0 No. 30930 *Radley* roared through Havant with the 11.30 a.m. Brighton to Plymouth train in full flight on 2.1.62. The Hayling platform and starting signal are on the right of the picture

In an attempt to eliminate steam traction from the line west of Brighton, Bulleid electric locomotives were tried out on the through train to Plymouth (the 11.30 a.m. from Brighton). The train had to be diverted to Fratton for engine changing purposes, but as it did not use the station no attempt was made to do away with the connecting carriages from Portsmouth & Southsea (which departed at 12.15 p.m. for coupling on to the main train at Fareham). C-C No. 20003 was the engine on a January day in 1964, surging along the straight track near Nutbourne with the Plymouth service. Within weeks steam had returned; even Standard 4MT 2-6-4Ts were pressed into use on the long haul to and from Salisbury

A rail tour that attracted a great deal of attention was the one headed by Alan Pegler's famous *Flying Scotsman* locomotive. Bought for preservation in 1963, No. 60103 was restored to LNER apple green livery with its original number, No. 4472, for rail tours all over the country. As the shadows lengthened over Havant station on 17.9.66, the sole surviving Gresley class A3 Pacific coasts into the up platform for a few moments before continuing the return journey to Victoria, via Chichester and the Brighton main line

The regular Salisbury to Chichester goods could usually be relied upon to produce a 4-6-0. By the 1960s the choice was becoming more limited and, in November 1963, it fell upon one of the handful fitted with six-wheel tender. No. 30837 was more often to be found at work between Reading and Redhill, but this time it took the coastal route making light of the substantial load on level track near Havant

Part 11 : The Brighton Influence on Hayling

At weekends during the summer there was a half-hourly service on the Hayling branch. As this could not be maintained on the usual basis with 'one engine in steam', additional stock had to be brought in on Saturdays and Sundays. On 22.7.62 'Terriers' Nos. 32646 and 32650 had brought up a second train from Fratton and were crossing over the main line at Havant, before setting back into the bay platform for the next departure to Hayling Island

The Hayling train steams out of Havant at 1.35 p.m. on 4.3.60 just as the 11.50 a.m. Waterloo to Portsmouth Harbour express powers through on the down fast line. The 11.50 was a restaurant car train that stopped only at Woking, Guildford and Haslemere (headcode '8') so any passengers for Hayling needed to catch the 11.27 a.m. from Waterloo to make the connection at Havant. Note the minor level-crossing in front of the water tower – its gates were controlled from the huge signal cabin to the right of Alx 0-6-0T No. 32661

On weekdays the branch timetable made provision for goods traffic: the first down train could be run as a 'mixed' as well as the 2.53 p.m. from Hayling (which was allowed extra time). The branch engine on 20.10.58 was class Alx 0-6-0T No. 32677 which brought the afternoon 'mixed' into the down main platform on arrival at Havant. This enabled the pick-up freight engine (class Q1 0-6-0 No. 33004) to buffer up to the rear of the train and remove the goods wagons before shunting them in the yard. No. 32677 was formerly at work on the Isle of Wight, being returned to the mainland in 1949 in malachite green livery. Note the extended bunker (all Isle of Wight engines had this) and bucket slung over a lamp iron

Rail fans said farewell to the Hayling line in spectacular fashion on 3.11.63. Not only were there *two* engines for the final special, but those selected happened to be the first Stroudley 'Terriers' ever built at the Brighton Works in 1872 and the oldest steam locomotives owned by British Railways. Spotless Alx tanks No. 32636 (formerly No. 72 *Fenchurch*) and No. 32670 (once No. 70 *Poplar*) took water at Havant before shuffling round into their correct positions with one engine at each end of the train. Both are now preserved, No. 32636 on the Bluebell and No. 32670 on the Kent & East Sussex Railway

On a bitterly cold day, 'Terrier' 0-6-0T No. 32661 lays a smoke screen as it brings the 2.53 p.m. 'mixed' up the hill from Langston towards Havant on 21.12.60. This diminutive engine spent many years at work on the Hayling line and retained the small bunker and tool box. Before this trip, the crew stacked up the coal to roof level and tied the weather sheeting over the cab door to deflect the wind

After spending some years in service stock, class Alx 0-6-0T No. 32650 was reinstated in capital stock for use on the Hayling branch. On 18.5.59 the full summer service of two train sets and three engines was in operation, and No. 32650 draws up at Langston with one of the half-hourly departures from Havant. The only level-crossing used by road traffic was situated here, and when the full service was provided the gates had to be opened (by hand) four times every hour. This had a major impact on road traffic which was frequently delayed here, especially at Bank Holiday weekends

Some indication of the relative sizes of a 'Terrier' locomotive and its carriages can be gained from this view at Hayling Island station, from the front compartment. Alx 0-6-0T No. 32661 has been given the road and begins to accelerate away towards Havant, while the fireman leans out of the cab to collect the token before the train ventures on to the single line. Note the pair of old LBSCR home signals: the main platform starter which suffered the ravages of time had to be replaced by an upper quadrant example on a new post, but the bay signal survived until closure in 1963

The very last train back from Hayling Island was headed by 'Terrier' No. 32670 (with No. 32636 bringing up the rear) on 3.11.63. It was a beautiful autumn day, the train was packed with people and hundreds more came to say goodbye to the little railway that had run across the impressive timber viaduct to Hayling for almost a century. There was a siding at this point, used during wartime for loading supplies in connection with D-Day, but in later years it provided a refuge for engineers' trains; the former train ferry to St Helens in the Isle of Wight had once been on the west side of the line here

Part 12 : Portsmouth Direct Line

After working a rail tour over the Gosport line, Class N 2-6-0 No. 31411 passed through Rowlands Castle on its way home to Guildford on 20.2.66. The signalbox and goods yard have since gone and the old-style lamps have been replaced by fluorescent lighting but otherwise the station has altered little in the intervening period

A break in the clouds highlights the boiler of a rebuilt 'Battle of Britain' Pacific No. 34052 *Lord Dowding* as it attacks the 1 in 100/110 approach to Buriton tunnel with a rail tour from London on 9.10.66. No regular steam-hauled passenger trains were scheduled over the Portsmouth Direct line during the hours of daylight, so any rail tour routed that way tended to attract patronage in the twilight years of this form of motive power

An uncommon pairing of 'West Country' Pacific locomotives occurred on 16.10.66 when No. 34019 *Bideford* and No. 34023 *Blackmore Vale* worked in tandem on a rail tour to Bournemouth via the Portsmouth Direct route. In this low-angle view the two Bulleid 'Spam-Cans' are glimpsed gathering speed on the descent from Buriton tunnel towards Havant

The centenary of the Portsmouth Direct line was marked by a special train, including Pullman cars, with suitable vintage engines. From Guildford to Gosport and back the rail tour was worked by a Drummond 'Black Motor' 0-6-0 built in 1897. After visiting the original LSWR terminus at Godalming, class 700 No. 30350 reached Petersfield at 1 p.m. on 25.1.59. The main station, footbridge and signalbox all remain in use today, but the old-style level-crossing gates have been replaced by lifting barriers and the trackwork has been simplified. All trace of the former bay platform for the Midhurst passenger trains has disappeared – it was opposite the signalbox, north of the level-crossing – and a new housing development has encroached on the old trackbed and Itshide siding beyond Tilmore bridge. Colour light signalling has replaced the semaphore arms, including the fine old LSWR lower quadrant starter shown in the foreground

Against a backcloth of leafless trees, and in stark contrast to the pristine snow, the last active Q1 0-6-0 (No. 33006) was shunting in the up goods yard at Haslemere on 19.1.66. Soon afterwards freight facilities were progressively withdrawn from the stations and yards along the Portsmouth Direct line so that, today, it relies solely upon passengers for its traffic

At a rarely photographed location, the 9.33 a.m. Portsmouth & Southsea to Surbiton parcels train races through on 20.12.65. Milford seldom seems to have featured in pictures and this view of the signalbox beside the level-crossing is now a matter of history – note how the building had been extended at some time. This parcels train was not a regular affair but only ran for a couple of weeks prior to Christmas, bringing the seasonal mail up from the coast. Class 4MT 4-6-0 No. 75068 was one of those engines fitted with double chimney and on this occasion was travelling very fast indeed

On 8.1.66 (with the benefit of advance notice) the author was able to observe the passage of a Saturday special from London to Exeter via the Portsmouth Direct route. Headed by 'West Country' Pacific, No. 34001 *Exeter*, the nine-coach train was whisked along at an electrifying pace at the foot of the 1 in 100 gradient between Godalming and Milford, parallel with the old Portsmouth Road (A3100), in damp and depressing winter weather

One of a handful of seasonal mail and parcels trains was noted outside Godalming on 16.12.65, with 4MT 4-6-0 No. 75068 in charge of an odd assortment of short wheelbase four-wheel vans pressed into use for this purpose, heading south for Portsmouth. While this may look like an ordinary goods train, the unusual position of the brake *next* to the engine tells its own story

Nine months after the official 'end of steam' on the Southern, two locomotives passed through Godalming under their own power on route to preservation – temporarily on the Longmoor Military Railway. Class 9F 2-10-0 No. 92203, once used on Saturday holiday trains over the Somerset & Dorset line to Bournemouth, had just been bought by wildlife and steam locomotive enthusiast David Shepherd. On 7.4.68 the renowned artist was on the footplate as this giant engine brought the unmistakeable sight, sound and smell of a steam locomotive back to Surrey for a few magic moments as it passed over the A3100 road near the Lake Hotel

The pride of the Longmoor Military Railway in its last years was the blue-liveried 2-10-0 No. 600 *Gordon* seen here steaming through Godalming station with a special to the interchange station at Liss on 16.4.66. It was very rare indeed for Longmoor engines to venture beyond their own system, and for one to appear on a passenger train was rarer still. The up platform shelter, with the distinctive angled roof, has been replaced by modern 'plastic' structures in recent years and the gas lighting has given way to fluorescents, but the main building has been retained

Only three months before the end of steam, Standard 5MT 4-6-0 No. 73115 was shunting at Godalming Goods (the original terminus before the Portsmouth Direct line was opened in 1859) while a train of 4-COR electric units streaks past on a Portsmouth Harbour to Waterloo express during the afternoon of 1.4.67

Opened on 15 October 1849 and closed to passengers from 1 May 1897, the Old Town station at Godalming – later known as Godalming Goods – remained in business for freight traffic until the end of the 1960s. On 31.3.67 a 'Crompton' diesel-electric Type 3 locomotive (D6546) stands beneath the canopy of the goods shed with Guildford's breakdown crane while a freight train is ready to leave

Crossing over on to the up line, 5MT 4-6-0 No. 73115 leaves Godalming Goods on its way back to Guildford shed on 1.4.67. Beyond can be seen the signal cabin and station at Farncombe, complete with ornate covered footbridge. Farncombe station was opened on 1 May 1897

with the demise of the last Q1 at Guildford shed, responsibility for the pick-up goods traffic over the Portsmouth Direct line fell to new electro-diesel locomotives. On 21.3.66 the up goods – a massive train with at least three brake vans – swept along the gentle downhill slope between Farncombe and Guildford behind No. E6014, in electric blue livery with white roof and small yellow warning panel; the headcode was '4B'

The signalman's view: the winter sunshine had succeeded in dispersing most of the early mist by the time class Q1 0-6-0 No. 33036 rattled past the Peasmarsh Junction 'box with the 9.33 a.m. pick-up goods from Haslemere to Guildford on 21.11.61. Beyond the bridge carrying the A3100 Old Portsmouth road over the main line a loading gauge keeps watch over a disused siding

Part 13 : Branch Lines to Midhurst

While passenger services to Midhurst were normally maintained by push–pull trains from their own platform opposite the signalbox at Petersfield, goods trains were assembled in the up yard to await departure from the loop platform at 1.35 p.m. On 22.1.55 the branch goods had class E5x 0-6-2T No. 32576 in charge, only a fortnight before closure. Note the quaint 'grab handles' on either side of the dome

After closure of the railway between Petersfield and Midhurst from 7.2.55, the only public transport was by bus. Southdown Motor Services operated two routes (Nos. 60 and 61) to Midhurst while the No. 60A served Nyewood, where Rogate station used to be. Southern Motorways (formerly Hants & Sussex) also ran a bus to Midhurst by way of some very minor roads, using ex-London Transport small capacity vehicles. In this typical sixties scene outside Petersfield station a Guy 'Special', with seats for twenty-six passengers, waits hopefully on the corner of Lavant Street; beyond, an Aldershot & District Dennis 'Loline' offers an alternative to the train on route 24 to Guildford

At 1.35 p.m. on Saturday, 5.2.55 the last 'Middy Goods' set out from Petersfield to Midhurst. Unlike the passenger trains, it did not appear to attract the attention of other photographers, so perhaps this may be the only record of it. 'Radial' 0-6-2T No. 32520 of class E4 was pulling only two or three wagons plus the brake when it was photographed, passing the old fixed distant signal at Mogg's Mede (about 1 mile from Petersfield station)

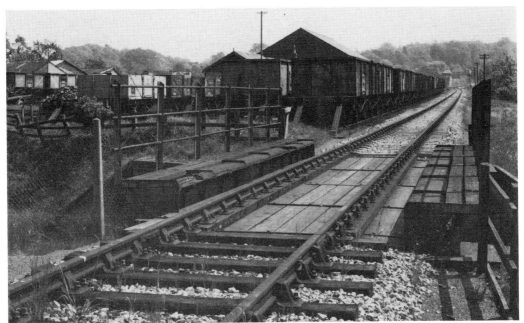

After closure of the branch from Petersfield in 1955 the track at Midhurst beyond Bepton Road bridge soon became rather overgrown, although the former LSWR goods yard and Midhurst Whites siding remained open. Before 1925 passenger trains from Petersfield terminated at the LSWR Midhurst Common station, but once the Bepton Road bridge had been strengthened all passenger traffic was concentrated at the LBSCR station. This view was taken in May 1959, when the main yard had a large number of goods wagons in the sidings. Midhurst was closed completely in the autumn of 1964

On a cold winter day the fireman was careful not to overfill E4 0-6-2T No. 32469 in case it should freeze. After shunting Midhurst yard on 21.12.60 the Billinton 'Radial' took the pick-up goods to Pulborough and on to Horsham. This particular engine was an old favourite at Horsham shed and often worked the Midhurst goods; the author can recall it deputizing for a failed M7 on a passenger turn to Petersfield in the early 1950s

After bringing the 'West Sussex Downsman' ramblers' excursion to Midhurst on 8.6.58 – the first passenger train since closure in February 1955 – the engine ran round its carriages and prepared to leave again. From the top of the tunnel the photographer had an unrivalled view as class Q 0-6-0 No. 30549 gave tongue, taking the empty stock back to Horsham for servicing. Set 472 was an eight-car rake of former LSWR 'Ironclad' corridors which had begun their journey from Charing Cross, reaching Midhurst via Epsom

On Christmas Eve 1960 the Midhurst goods had a few loaded wagons of sugar beet to go back to Horsham yard. In very damp conditions class E4 0-6-2T No. 32557 brings the train into Midhurst station before plunging into the tunnel on its eastbound journey. The station building remained intact until the whole site was redeveloped as a housing estate some years after total closure in 1964

By the end of 1961 the E4 0-6-2Ts were nearing retirement on BR. A rather forlorn No. 32474, with a chalked MOT sign on the smokebox, waits to leave Midhurst yard with the goods on 27.12.61. The preceding number in the class, No. 32473, was sold to the Bluebell Railway and used by them in lined black livery for a time before restoration in Brighton umber as *Birch Grove*

The 12.30 p.m. Midhurst pick-up goods leaves a trail of smoke in the air as it passes Selham behind E4 0-6-2T No. 32469, 21.12.60. The yard at Selham was only scheduled to be shunted by trains bound for Midhurst, so wagons intended for transfer to Pulborough and beyond had to go on to the terminus and come out again

With a liberal coating of soot and grime, class C2x 'Vulcan' No. 32534 draws to a halt at Petworth with the Midhurst branch freight on 16.6.61. Despite closure of the line to passengers more than six years before, the station nameboard still stands in its appointed place

One could wait for years at this spot to get the right combination. Sometimes the engine ran tender-first, often the weather was indifferent and, by the autumn of 1961, the availability of a 'Vulcan' was becoming a problem. On 23.10.61 everything came together, as this study of C2x 0-6-0 No. 32549 proves. Some years earlier, No. 32549 had been fitted with one of the double-domed boilers. These were used indiscriminately by classes E5x, E6x and C2x after the demise of the C3 type for which it had been developed. This picture was taken on what was to be the last occasion on which the author saw a 'Vulcan' on the Midhurst goods, leaving the eastern portal of the tunnel on its way to Pulborough

Before withdrawal of passenger services, it was only rarely that a Q or Q1 0-6-0 traversed the Midhurst line. After the last 'Vulcan' went for scrap and class E4 'Radial' tanks were hard to come by, there was little choice in the matter. On 22.6.62 class Q No. 30545 had charge of the 12.30 p.m. Midhurst to Pulborough pick-up goods, pausing briefly at Fittleworth before continuing along the single track to Hardham Junction. A solitary 16T mineral wagon stood in the tiny goods yard, soon to be closed. The River Rother sometimes burst its banks and flooded the track here during winter

Before shunting could take place in the yard at Petworth, the single line token had to be used to 'open' the ground frame. On 4.7.60 class E4 'Radial' tank No. 32470 blows off impatiently while the proper ritual is observed. The lovely timber station here became derelict for some years after total closure in May 1966, but has since been restored as a private house

Nicknamed 'Jinxy', the last double-domed class C2x 'Vulcan' No. 32535 trundles the Midhurst goods through Fittleworth on its way back to Pulborough on 30.7.61. This useful, and interesting, type of locomotive was taken out of service at the end of January 1962

Part 14 : Three Bridges to Tunbridge Wells (West)

Rowfant station was delightful; although a passing place on a single track railway, it was very rural, having a most attractive station and signalbox. Class H 0-4-4T no. 31551 accelerates away with its push–pull set (602) towards Three Bridges during the afternoon of 14.3.62. For much of the day there was an hourly service in each direction between Three Bridges and East Grinstead

Appearances can be deceptive, for at first glance one might think that this was a two-coach diesel train entering Rowfant station. It turned out to be a steam push–pull outfit with set 602 being propelled from the rear by H 0-4-4T No. 31530, forming an afternoon shuttle service between Three Bridges and East Grinstead on 22.1.62. While diesel trains did take over this duty in due course, under the Beeching plan the line was closed from 2.1.67. How much more sense it would have made to electrify it, especially now that the third rail has been extended from Sanderstead to East Grinstead. Even if semaphore signals and hand-operated level-crossing gates were eliminated, Rowfant's pretty station could have remained in business

As the winter sunlight fades, a LBSCR veteran plods through Grange Road with a goods from Tunbridge Wells (West) to Three Bridges. 'Vulcan' 0-6-0 No. 32523 was one of the last three examples of the C2x type to remain at work, and this could perhaps have been one of its final duties on 22.1.62; it was sent for scrap at the end of that month

In happier times a 'Vulcan' might be seen on a passenger turn. On 12.9.50, class C2x 0-6-0 No. 32546 waits for the 'right away' from Grange Road station with the 2.39 p.m. from Three Bridges to Tunbridge Wells (West) service. Though the signal cabin was similar to that at Rowfant, the station buildings were completely different

R.C. Riley

With curiously assorted coaches, Billinton class D3 0-4-4T No. 32390 propels its push–pull train out of Forest Row station towards the setting sun on 12.9.50. This engine proved to be the last surviving LBSCR four-coupled passenger tank in normal use, working all over Sussex as well as up to East Croydon and out to Guildford; it was scrapped in 1955

R.C. Riley

102

On Sunday, 13.6.65 'The Wealdsman' rail tour brought a double-headed special train to a number of Sussex lines due to close the following day. With 'Mogul' No. 31803 (U-class) leading N 2-6-0 No. 31411, the pair thundered through Withyham on their way to Hastings via the 'Cuckoo Line'. Note the abandoned goods yard in the foreground

A classic impression of Tunbridge Wells (West) station in its heyday is given by this scene of 16.3.57. A German-built L 4-4-0 No. 31771 pulls out with a train for Brighton while an Eastbourne service waits its turn behind an unidentified Fairburn (LMR) 4MT 2-6-4T in the adjoining platform
R.C. Riley

The last scheduled passenger train to be steam hauled between Tunbridge Wells (West) and Eastbourne was given a subdued send-off by a handful of railwaymen on 12.6.65; passenger traffic between Eridge and Hailsham (exclusive) was withdrawn the following day. 4MT 2-6-4T No. 80144 is steaming well as it starts the train in characteristic style, but another chapter was closed for the railways of Sussex. The West station closed in the 1980s

Part 15 : From Sanderstead to the Sea

The steam-hauled 5.40 p.m. from London Bridge was as important to commuters in the fifties as corresponding electric services are today. It ran from East Croydon via Oxted, East Grinstead and the Bluebell line to Lewes before terminating at Brighton some 2½ hrs later. On 23.6.54 a new Standard 4MT 2-6-4T heads the train as it was photographed at Woldingham; No. 80086 was being 'run in', returning to Brighton where it had been built earlier in the month. It was allocated to Bury in Lancashire shortly after

R.C. Riley

Oxted remains an important junction long after the days of steam. On 12.7.62 Standard 4MT 2-6-4T No. 80144 takes water after arrival with the 1.08 p.m. from London (Victoria). After providing a connection for the Ashurst line, the main train continued to Tunbridge Wells (West) via East Grinstead and Forest Row

The signal cabin at Oxted retained much of its charm, as can be seen in this view taken on 5.3.67. It is clear from the truncated water column on the down platform that the age of steam had already passed here, but use of 'West Country' 4-6-2 No. 34102 Lapford for a rail tour ensured sufficent reserves

By 1967 the choice of motive power for rail tours was becoming rather limited. The 'Surrey Downsman' on 5 March that year saw a filthy Standard 4MT 4-6-0 pressed into service on the eight-coach special as it passed Oxted heading north for East Croydon. The three-way point in the goods yard is worthy of note

On a fine spring evening, H 0-4-4T No. 31320 propels its ex-LSWR corridor push–pull set out of
Ashurst station forming the 6.09 p.m. from Oxted to Tunbridge Wells (West), 17.4.54. This
fascinating study reveals the home signal with a sighting board, gas lighting and canopy supports
still painted in wartime colours

R.C. Riley

Eridge station was a four-platform junction, with the main building constructed at street level
above the tracks. On 26.4.65 when diesel-electric unit 1305 was departing on a service to Lewes,
steam services were rare in this area. Another diesel unit stands in the adjoining platform
providing a connection to Eastbourne via the 'Cuckoo Line', which was due to close on 14 June

Amid unspoiled woodland, Standard class 4MT 2-6-4T No. 80140 clips along under light regulator with an Eastbourne to Tunbridge Wells train between Rotherfield & Mark Cross and Eridge one fine evening in July 1964. The 'Cuckoo Line' had less than a year left in service

As the shadows lengthen, Standard 4MT No. 80142 restarts its train of 'slimline' Maunsell carriages from the picturesque Rotherfield & Mark Cross station on the 'Cuckoo Line' to Eastbourne on a summer's evening in July 1964. Electric lighting had been installed here in Southern Railway days, but such confidence in the future evaporated during the 1960s

For the last time steam emerged from the murky depths of Heathfield tunnel when U No. 31803 and N No. 31411 brought 'The Wealdsman' rail tour into the station on 13 June 1965. It was also the last train to travel the entire length of the 'Cuckoo Line', for from the junction south of Eridge (Redgate Mill junction) all traffic was withdrawn as far as Hailsham; the line to Polegate stayed open for another three years

A work-weary 4MT tank, No. 80033, hisses into Mayfield station heading for Eastbourne, 6.5.65. By this time Bulleid stock was in use on the 'Cuckoo Line' on those services not already handed over to diesel traction

On 24.6.62 Heathfield witnessed another double-headed rail tour when an all-LSWR team powered the special on its return from Eastbourne. Class M7 0-4-4T No. 30055 piloted the preserved 'Greyhound' class T9 4-4-0 No. 120 up through the South Downs, and the immaculate pair of Drummond veterans made a fine spectacle in the mid-summer sunshine as they passed Heathfield signalbox

Some 'Cuckoo Line' trains passing at Horam station – an establishment that had been blessed with other titles in its time. On 26.4.65 the green painted diesel unit 1308 was bound for Eridge while the down train to Eastbourne consisted of a set of Mk. I carriages (No. 537) hauled by Standard 2-6-4T No. 80142. Note the tail lamp hung at the rear of the DMU

Apart from the yard at Hailsham, all intermediate freight traffic was abandoned over the 'Cuckoo Line' in its final years. On 12.5.65 a short train of mineral wagons made their way north from Eastbourne through Horam behind a shabby Standard tank (No. 80019), while on the right of the picture evidence of the recent lifting of the goods sidings in readiness for total closure the following month can be seen. One of the first BR-designed tank engines to be built at Brighton Works in 1951, was No. 80019 and it survived until the final months of Southern steam in 1967

Once noted for its private electric railway to the nearby hospital, Hellingly station presented a rather forlorn sight on 6.5.65. Standard 4MT No. 80034 paused here with an Eastbourne to Tunbridge Wells (West) service, when the fireman's efforts to make up the fire effectively blacked out the building

It was a bright, sunny day on 26.4.65, six weeks before closure of the 'Cuckoo Line', but that meant difficulty in taking photographs against the light – this record of 4MT 2-6-4T No. 80011 under the canopy of platform 1 at Eastbourne illustrates the problem. Other hazards were the energized conductor rails and a string of coal wagons on the other side of the train. No. 80011 ran chimney-first back to Tunbridge Wells; it was transferred to Bournemouth shed shortly afterwards where it lasted to the very end of steam on the Southern, being withdrawn in July 1967

The only line still open south of Eridge today terminates at Uckfield, the remainder (via Isfield and Barcombe Mills) to Lewes was closed in 1969. In steam days Crowborough station looked like this, with Standard tank No. 80013 in the down platform with a Tunbridge Wells (West) to Lewes local which, in turn, would become the 4.11 p.m. to London (Victoria), 2.9.53

R.C. Riley

An impressive panorama of Lewes station could be obtained from above the south signalbox. On this occasion a 'Mickey Mouse' 2MT 2-6-2T, No. 41296, is starting away with a former SECR 'Birdcage' set showing headcode discs which indicate the Oxted line via Eridge

R.C. Riley

Steam-hauled trains from Brighton towards Lewes were faced with the challenge of Falmer bank. A most unlikely combination in the opposite direction approached Falmer station with a rail tour from Newhaven to Brighton on 7.10.62, with the ninety-year-old 'Terrier' 0-6-0T No. 32636 being dwarfed by Billinton E6 0-6-2T No. 32418 as they coast downhill through the cutting

Occasional special passenger trains were run from Brighton over the Kemp Town branch. Closed for ordinary passenger traffic in 1933, it remained open for goods long after – providing an excellent venue for periodic rail tours. On 23.6.56 the Brighton works shunter, No. 377S, brought a pair of antique push–pull carriages to Kemp Town, the 'Terrier's' exhaust still drifting out of the tunnel under the Downs while the train drew up at the platform. No. 377S had been transferred to departmental stock when class A1 *Boxhill* retired in 1946, being repainted in Stroudley's distinctive livery of improved engine green. In its last years it was given the BR number No. 32635, but retained its colourful paintwork until withdrawal

Part 16 : Brighton Main Line

In the absence of more familiar motive power on the Brighton line – K 2-6-0s or 'C2x' 0-6-0s, for example – one of the last active examples of Maunsell's Q class had to be pressed into service one overcast day in the summer of 1964. No. 30543 plods through Horley with a trainload of 'Palvans' in the direction of Brighton. The original Horley station was replaced by the present one in 1905

Bank Holiday weekends in the fifties and sixties were good times to see railway excursions at South Coast resorts. On 20.5.56, Whit Sunday, the fine weather brought out the crowds – and the trains. The empty stock of a ten-coach excursion from Rugby was pulled slowly away from the arrival platform by a commendably clean M7 0-4-4T (No. 30108), emulating the feats performed by similar engines in and out of Waterloo throughout the fifties. This particular engine had seen service on Petersfield–Midhurst–Pulborough push–pull services before supension of passenger traffic in 1955, and was more used to two-coach trains

Last of the line, ex-SECR L class 4-4-0 No. 31780 stands forlorn and forgotten outside Brighton station on 10.6.61, waiting to be broken up for scrap. Scarcely more than a year later, the most powerful 4-4-0s ever built – the 'Schools' class – would be ekeing out their final days, too. In the 1960s there seemed to be no place for graceful four-coupled steam engines like these

One rather unexpected victim of the Beeching cuts was the electrified branch between Haywards Heath and Horsted Keynes. While the logical step might have been to electrify from Sanderstead to East Grinstead (as has now happened) and continue the third-rail through Kingscote and West Hoathly to Horsted Keynes, so completing another of the Southern's favoured 'loops', the 4¾-mile branch was axed in October 1963. On 1.4.62 the local service from Horsted Keynes was provided by a pair of 2-BIL units, with No. 2147 leading as they slid silently away from Ardingly (the only intermediate station on the branch)

116

Shortly after the departure of the electric service, visiting class J52 (ex-GNR J13) 0-6-0ST No. 1247 puffed sedately through Ardingly with a returning 'Blue Belle' excursion on 1.4.62. This former Great Northern saddle tank, BR No. 68846, had been purchased and restored privately in the late-1950s, but it is still remarkable to think that it was allowed to take the special train unaided between London, Haywards Heath and Horsted Keynes, and back. The elderly Stirling engine appears to be being urged on by supporters in the guard's compartment of the Maunsell Boat Train brake as it headed for Copyhold Junction

Freshly restored to LSWR pea green livery, the 1885-built Adams 'Radial' 4-4-2T No. 488 darkens the sky as it pulls the BR 'Blue Belle' excursion stock out of Haywards Heath station towards Copyhold Junction, Ardingly and Horsted Keynes on 31.3.63. Set 212 had flat-sided boat train brakes at either end of the rake. As BR No. 30583, this engine had retired from the Lyme Regis branch only two years earlier

Before the link via Ardingly was severed, one last 'Blue Belle' special rail tour was run from London on 15.9.63. In this scene at Haywards Heath after the arrival of the excursion are some of the most intriguing contrasts ever to be found on British Railways in the 1960s: 4-SUB electric unit No. 4726 is leaving for Brighton with a stopping service from London while, across the platform, stand two veterans from the Victorian age. Caledonian Railway 4-2-2 No. 123 is coupled ahead of 'Greyhound' T9 4-4-0 No. 120 in LSWR livery, both engines waiting for an opportunity to continue southward to Brighton for servicing and turning in preparation for the return journey to London. Note the orderly crowds on platforms and lineside

In the fading light, the camera records a magic moment at Haywards Heath on 21.10.62. With the last surviving Adams' class 0415 'Radial' 488 leading LBSCR 'Terrier' No. 55 *Stepney* on a train of Southern excursion stock from Horsted Keynes, class T9 4-4-0 No. 120 waits alongside, ready to attach itself to the front of the train for the return to London. The Alx 0-6-0T is painted in Stroudley's colourful improved engine green while the two LSWR engines are in pea green livery – and all this on third-rail electrified track on the Brighton Main Line

Watched by vast crowds, Caledonian 'Single' No. 123 and T9 4-4-0 No. 120 makes a stately exit from Haywards Heath with the returning 'Blue Belle' excursion on 15.9.63. The sight and sound of these two grand old engines carefully crossing the electrified junctions at the end of a perfect day must be indelibly etched on the memories of all who were present

Making a most dramatic smokescreen as it approaches Cooksbridge, Brighton class H2 **Atlantic** No. 32425 *Trevose Head* is going at full speed with the 5.48 p.m. up boat train from **Newhaven** Harbour to Victoria on a summer's day in the early 1950s. The train would join the Brighton **main** line at Keymer Junction, just south of Haywards Heath

R.C. Riley

Part 17 : The Hastings Line and Branches

Reminiscent of the days before Hastings diesel-electric multiple units took over passenger traffic, a brace of inside-cylinder 4-4-0s thunder through Etchingham with a returning rail tour on 11.6.61. Class D1 No. 31749 is seen here leading L1 No. 31786 towards Tunbridge Wells (Central) at speed

Although the Kent & East Sussex line had closed to passengers in 1954, freight traffic was maintained between Robertsbridge and Tenterden (Town) until 1961. After that, it closed completely except for a few hundred yards out of Robertsbridge, where occasional wagons were shunted to and from Hodson's Mill. The mill purchased their own steam engine from BR – ex-SECR P 0-6-0T No. 31556 that had been based at Brighton – and collected the odd wagon with it from Robertsbridge yard. One such foray was made during May 1964, when the tiny locomotive puffed along the weed-infested track towards the mill with a single wagon

Still bearing signs of its former ownership, P class 0-6-0T No. 31556 puffs across the A21 trunk road on the outskirts of Robertsbridge for a rare outing to the nearby BR station to collect a wagon for Hodson's Mill in May 1964. It was thanks to the mill's purchase of this engine that it survived long enough to be acquired, ultimately, by the revived Kent & East Sussex Railway and restored to traffic in the 1980s

The end of BR traffic on the Kent & East Sussex line was marked in style, with a special train and an engine at either end. 'Terrier' No. 32662 headed the rail tour out of Robertsbridge, and is seen crossing an ungated road whilst climbing towards Tenterden on 11.6.61. As No. 662 *Martello*, it has since been restored to LBSCR livery at Bressingham Gardens, Norfolk

Crowhurst station was the junction for the 4½-mile branch to Bexhill West. On 25.7.53 a smart L1 4-4-0 No. 31783 is seen arriving at the down platform with a Charing Cross to Hastings train, as the service from Bexhill stood in the bay on the up side with class D3 0-4-4T No. 32384 in charge. Across on the opposite side of the station H 0-4-4T No. 31274 waits to propel set 660, an ex-SECR train, to Bexhill West after passengers from London had boarded

R.C. Riley

A highly appropriate choice for the last BR excursion to Tenterden on 11.6.61, class A1x 0-6-0T No. 32670 had been sold to the K & ESR in 1901 as their No. 3 *Bodiam*. It was taken into BR stock on nationalization in 1948 and operated at several different locations until 1963, when it was purchased for preservation. In this picture, No. 32670 is entering Northiam station with the rail tour, assisted in the rear by No. 32662. As the Kent & East Sussex Railway reopens more of its track, maybe this 1872-built 'Terrier' will reach Northiam again in the 1990s

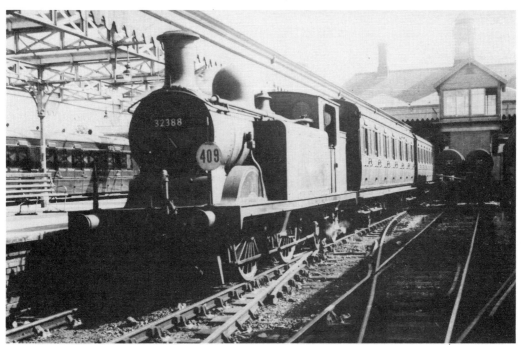

The terminal station of Bexhill West, though only at the end of a 4½-mile branch from Crowhurst, was quite an impressive structure. In this scene from the early days of nationalization, class D3 0-4-4T No. 32388 and auto-train stand waiting for the next journey to Crowhurst, while a newly-repainted push–pull set can be seen on the other side of the platform

R.C. Riley

Part 18 : Under New Management – Steam Revival

A 1980s glimpse of the Kent & East Sussex Railway at Rolvenden station, with 0-6-0ST *Northiam* about to leave with a train from Wittersham Road to Tenterden. Now numbered 25, this modern saddle tank was built by Hunslet in 1953 for the Ministry of Defence; it was numbered 197 and latterly based at Bicester before disposal and preservation

Even under new management, the Bluebell line has had its closures. On 1.4.62 a new halt was opened at Holywell Waterworks by Dr Beeching, but it was closed again on 31.10.63 and subsequently dismantled. On opening day in 1962, the returning 'Blue Belle' excursion passes Holywell Halt without stopping, with the restored Adams 4-4-2T No. 488 leading and GNR saddletank No. 1247 bringing up the rear

The only example of its class to have escaped from scrap, 'Q' 0-6-0 No. 541 has been painstakingly restored to its original livery of the pre-war Southern Railway period. It has been an ideal 'maid of all work' – this timeless picture at Horsted Keynes was taken in the eighties

Under a dramatic sky, the Bluebell's first engine, 'Alx' 0-6-0T No. 55 *Stepney* (built in 1875) takes the lead past Freshfield Halt with the 'Blue Belle' rail tour of 1.4.62; GNR 0-6-0ST No. 1247 was assisting at the rear, having brought the special train all the way from London on its own. Freshfield Halt remains in use, and has proved popular with photographers over many years

Back to the future? From the footplate of former SECR class P 0-6-0T No. 27 (then named *Primrose*) on 21.10.62 the line ahead was blocked at Horsted Keynes. But in the 1990s? Having been successful in a long drawn-out planning appeal, the Bluebell Railway has begun to extend northwards towards East Grinstead. Although much hard work lies ahead, Kingscote station is being restored and new track will be laid to reinstate a connection with British Rail one day. Instead of being a terminus in the middle of the Sussex Weald, Horsted Keynes is likely to become an important passing place on a 10-mile line from Sheffield Park to East Grinstead